Let Me Fucking Cry

Let Me Fucking Cry

Rhiannon Janae

This book is dedicated to:

All those treading through waves of grief.
Keep swimming, your shore is awaiting.

To the boy whom I first loved,
I hope you have found the peace you could not find
on this earth.

And lastly to my mother, who has gifted me with
this creative hand. I hope you are smiling down on
me proudly.

'Trigger Warning'

This book talks about mental illness, grief, death, substance abuse, depression, and abuse.

This is an extremely vulnerable experience.

The intention of this publication is to help others find comfort in the imperfections.

Queens don't wear crowns.
They wear grief inside their bones and scars on their
hearts.

Who/what are you grieving?

_____

_____

_____

_____

_____

_____

_____

_____

_____

_____

_____

_____

_____

_____

_____

_____

_____

_____

_____

_____

_____

_____

_____

The Denial...............................17

The Anger.............................63

The Bargaining.........................105

The Depression.......................149

The Acceptance.......................203

The Denial

Let Me Fucking Cry

The ironic thing about death is
once it happens,
the world continues,
but yours stops

forever.

A deadly kiss.

The day I let your lips caress mine, I knew at that moment; I was forever yours and that I would never be able to get your taste out of my mouth.

-lip-sticking

The scariest thing about me is that I was in love with the one thing that scares me the most. Danger. I found loopholes to continue to love the one who had already ruined me. I tended not to see the reality of my past; and maybe it was because somewhere deep down inside of me, I believed I deserved it. I thought I deserved a love that was only capable of taking, while all I did was give. I loved the way it made me feel hopeless; all while feeling hopelessly in love. I was addicted to the thrill and chaos that filled our home. I loved the things that were toxic because I knew they were not good for me, and that made me want them even more.

Your hands feel like the home I have always been looking for.

Why do you feel like home, yet you have no roof?

Why do you feel safe, yet your hands are full of harm?

Why am I always chasing after someone who was never here to begin with?

Let Me Fucking Cry

If you are so bad for me,
then why do you taste so good?

-sweet taste of poison

Rhiannon Janae

I cannot escape him.
Not because he will not let me,
but because I will not let me.

He is like a drug I do not need,
but desperately want.

It is like my heart was made to break in his
hands and shatter all over myself in a
masterpiece of unrequited love.

-love addict

Let Me Fucking Cry

Blue daises rot in our bedroom corner. The bedroom I grew up in, where I would starve my bones at the curse of my mother's co-dependent love for me. The room where I wrote how much I loved a boy whom I did not even know because I was too scared to feel something, or anything. The room where my best friend and I would sing every note off key to our favorite songs, as we poured our hearts out through the lyrics. The room I used to feel safe in has now turned into a quarantine filled with your disease. The bedroom we fuck in every night as you swear, I am the only one for you; damn-well knowing you are going to break my heart again in the morning.

-childhood bedroom

Rhiannon Janae

It is cold tonight.

The power is out,
because we cannot afford to turn it back on.

Thankfully, there are plenty of candles to light so we
can watch each other drink cheap vodka as I try not
to get sick from the taste of it.

Thank God for my mother's excessive love for
candles, or I would not be able to see your face past
nightfall.

I think this is getting to be too much for me.

We are living in filth, and now darkness.

I get worried when I cannot see you because I fear
you will disappear forever.
Will that happen one day from all the darkness that
burrows inside of you?

It is scary to see what is happening inside of us as
we watch the shadows from the glow of the candles
dance on these walls.

Let Me Fucking Cry

I swear they are trying to tell me something.

I don't know if it is all the vodka, or the exhaustion
of trying to keep you alive every day,
but I swear these walls are speaking.

-how we look in the shadows

I have washed my hands of you, but there's still bruising at the tips of my fingers so that everything I touch still bathes in your taste. I am never fully cleansed of you since you have branded my body like a hot metal rod to the skin; constantly reminding me of who claimed me first.

- ~~own~~ *me*

There is a difference between wants and needs.

I do not want you,

but I do need you.

-codependency

I have let my body attach itself to these sheets all week. I have become one with this mattress, just like I used to become one with you on top of this mattress. I hate that I took your skin brushing up against mine for granted. I hate that I didn't savor the taste of your lips somewhere inside my mouth. I hate that these walls that enclose me had once enclosed you. I hate that you can see me, yet I cannot see you.

Let Me Fucking Cry

The funny thing is,
we are all so scared of abandonment,
yet we abandon ourselves so easily.

-running from the things we need the most

Rhiannon Janae

*Wrap your finger around mine and promise me that
this is our year. We have gotten this far; and though
my love for you is tainted, every time you walk into
the room, my heart races. So, that tells me it still
beats for you. Just please assure me that the last time
will be what it already is:*

the last time.

*I know I can still love you because that is all I
wanted this whole time. But I do not know how
much longer my heart can take another "next time".*

*Because if you leave again, the next time you walk
into the room my heart may not beat for you,
knowing you will only leave us again.*

-detox

Let Me Fucking Cry

Green eyes
and purple words
that left
markings on my body.

Too thin.
Too fat.
Never quite enough.

Our love felt rotten,
yet still edible.
Even though it made me sick,
I still bit into it.

-bad apple

My best friend has become the one thing I always run back to. Loneliness. I cannot get enough of it. I prefer to be close to only one thing at a time. I like to feel the embrace of how bitter I have become inside. I like to be reminded of all my hauntings so I can write more of these pages. I have become a version of myself that I both envy and despise. A love/ hate. The kind of feeling I am used to. Loving something so much, while hating it even more. I am now the person I once feared, which gives me hope that I am becoming better at facing my fears.

I quit smoking because it reminded me of how your lips would taste in the mornings. How after every exhale of nicotine, I no longer had someone to pass the next inhale to. That made my days harder, and I am desperate for any relief I can get. Everyone keeps telling me you are all around me; in the air, trees, clouds, and flowers. Maybe that is why I keep burrowing myself inside this shitty apartment, because I don't want to just feel you, I want to see you. Because believing is seeing to me; and if I cannot see you, how do I know you are there? If you are all around me, then why do I feel utterly and miserably alone?

Rhiannon Janae

I was a painting on his canvas.

Stroking me the way he wanted.
Dressing me the way he wanted.

So I could become a portrait of a woman
he could show off
for others to envy,
and for me to despise.

-one to marvel at

Let Me Fucking Cry

All the words we never got to say; and all the ways I will have to learn how to say them to someone else.

-words you never got to hear

You left me here; in this dusty bed, wearing mold on the shower curtain. The telephone doesn't ring, because no one is looking for me. The tv only plays people trying to sell me shit, but at night you can watch others fucking. Why do I stay here? I do not feel safe, but I do not feel unsafe. I think that is what our love feels like. Almost like a numbness until you leave me, and then I feel crazy, as if I cannot breathe. But that's what gets me. The fact that I fear being without you, all while being with you, is a horror show. Watching you fill yourself up with drugs, as you disappear into darkness. All the things that would make someone want to run. But here I sit; calm, in a shitty motel, staring at the cigarette-stained ceiling waiting for your return. I look at the door knowing that if I leave, I would be opening something that has been closed for so long. The door hides all the pain I have locked up. The pain that brought us together and keeps us here. The pain that allows me to continue to think your love is all that I deserve. The pain that keeps me at a standstill and never gets me ahead. Maybe treading in these waters is safe. Yes, I am tired, but I know how this works. Opening the door is too unknown. This is familiar. Why is the mind so fucked up, that it makes you believe you deserve nothing good? Why can't I get my legs to walk out of here and be young and free of this nightmare? Why do I stay here waiting for someone who cannot love me? Maybe it is because what I truly fear is myself.

Why do I love everything more when I cannot have it?

Let Me Fucking Cry

Regret keeps her awake
and remorse wakes her up in the morning.

Regret for staying another day,
remorse for doing it all again in the morning.

-the morning after

Rhiannon Janae

I hate the way my stomach feels when I wake up in the morning. It is like a mountain of grief has burrowed inside of me; sitting there, preparing itself to hibernate. It is spring now. Time to see the flowers bloom and hear the birds sing. But the grief will not let me. It sits in my stomach hibernating until something impossible happens; you return. I must tell my stomach every morning that you are not returning, and that I am no longer the girl I once was as yours. That it is time to become the girl I am supposed to be on my own. Maybe one morning my stomach will be able to handle it.

-*growing pains.*

Let Me Fucking Cry

Butterfly kisses were the way we got lost in each other's eyes.

I drink pumpkin beer in the fall now, because of that one night you were home. We sat on the front porch, it was chilly, so I wore your flannel. You smiled that night and I remember thinking about how I wanted to pause and stay in that moment forever. Because you looked so happy for a second there, and I hope I had something to do with that. But now all I have is the spice of pumpkin hitting my lips as the leaves fall off the trees, dying just a little bit inside with every taste.

-the october blues

Let Me Fucking Cry

*How can someone become everything and nothing
all at the same time?*

*How can one person make you feel the happiest and
then the saddest within the same hour?*

*How can someone give so much, just to take it
away?*

*How can I want you to leave so badly, but need you
to stay even more?*

You moved inside my heart when we were
twenty-two.

They call it young love,
but it was a love like I never knew before.

Is it all the same for everyone?

Are we all haunted by the one we let inside us
first?

Ever since, I have had my locks changed.

-virginity

Let Me Fucking Cry

I have carried you so far
that my hands are bruised
and my legs ache.
In the hopes that if I carry us far enough,
you will no longer need my legs to stand.

Rhiannon Janae

Maybe it is okay if this ruins me because it will
make all the battles worth fighting for.

-battlegrounds

Let Me Fucking Cry

Today I decided I missed you a lot.
I went and drank too many glasses of wine.
One by one until one of them made me forget.

Most of them did until they made me
remember
all too well.

They rumbled inside of me like a gun, just
waiting to be triggered.
And when I pulled the trigger, out came all the
hate inside of me.

The hate of missing you.
The hate of loving you.
The hate of losing you.
The hate of losing me.

Maybe all that's inside of me is hate, and that's
why I want to escape myself so badly.

I'm like a gun just waiting to be triggered.

-on automatic

Rhiannon Janae

Putting one foot in front of the other on days like these is a test of my strength. Because lately, I have been finding myself underneath bubble baths and junk food. Or uncovering myself at shitty dive bars, drinking liquor that does not agree with my body. I leave myself on days like these, when the grief becomes too much for my heart to bear. So, I put it on my liver. Sometimes I find the most peace in the most uncomfortable situations because it is in those moments that I feel most like myself. It is the discomfort that keeps me comforted, because then maybe if I look hard enough, I can find you there.

-alcohol-infused

If those walls could have talked, they would have said,

"You are too young to be this damaged from a man who can't even get a grip on himself."

"You are too smart to think the love you deserve is in the hands of a man who can't even hold himself together long enough to stand on his own two feet."

"You are too good to let some guy who doesn't even love himself make you feel so unloved."

If those walls could have talked, would I have listened?

You never wanted anyone else to have me,
and if I keep going on like this,

I am scared you might get your way.

Let Me Fucking Cry

I am here once again, sitting on this wooden bench, chugging endless glasses of cheap wine that will surely make my head hurt in the morning. But I swear every sip brings me closer to you. This death I feel that keeps me in a constant trance of sitting in a shitty dive bar as I play the same song repeatedly on the jukebox. I hope you can hear me crying in the form of these sad lyrics. This might be hell, but nothing can save me now.

-purgatory

Today I thought about you, and if you were still here and had gotten better. What if we had gotten the house with the white picket fence and the wrap-around porch that I had dreamt of? What if my body had kept our children safe and able to grow? You would cook us dinner at night as I bathed the kids. And all those ugly ways we treated one another evaporated and became delusional daydreams in my head, just like this one.

-miscarried opportunity

Maybe part of me does not want to fully heal because the hurt has become so creative. My muse is my pain and without it, what kind of words would live inside of me? Pain holds memories and those memories mold me into who I am, and who I will become. I do not want to become my pain, but I want to remember it so I can try to find a way for it all to make sense.

-piecing together the broken puzzle

Rhiannon Janae

I have never loved someone before you and I keep feeling like I will never love someone after you. But if I let that happen, I fear you might win. Because when you took my heart, you carved your initials inside of it so that any lover after you would never have my whole heart. Or if they did, they would be reminded of who was here first.

-ex *marks the spot*

Let Me Fucking Cry

Learning how to let you go,
and let me in.

Rhiannon Janae

Falling in love scares me
because it reminds me of you.
I know it sounds tainted
and trust me, I want to think of love as
something warming.
But at the end of the day, love is what broke
me.
Whether it was too much of it,
or not enough
is something I am still trying to figure out.

Let Me Fucking Cry

I am a river that
runs
in
your
waters.

Though I drown,
I like the way
you hold me under.

-denial river

What is causing your denial?

_____

_____

_____

_____

_____

_____

_____

_____

_____

_____

_____

_____

_____

_____

_____

_____

_____

_____

_____

_____

_____

_____

_____

_____

_____

The Anger

Why have I fallen so weak into the hands of someone I cannot even call a man? Because a real man means what he says when he says, *"Next time will be different."*

But here, each time is the same phrase ending with another false hope from the repetition of *next time.*

The only time it ever changed profoundly was when the universe gave us no *next time.*

That is when it became different.

Our love was becoming a game of who could hurt each other more.

You always won.

-checkmate

Let Me Fucking Cry

I gave into my stubbornness and decided to start going to therapy.

And what I had feared, happened.

I started to hate you.

Rhiannon Janae

We became cursed the moment you tied your finger around mine.

-pinky promise

Let Me Fucking Cry

Today I hate you.

I hate the way I let you keep creeping inside of me with the parts of you that you let everyone else have a piece of.

Today I hate you.

I hate the way I let your filthy lies coax my ears to give you another year of myself under your arm.

Today I hate you.

I hate the way I let you fool me into losing everyone who loved me by making me believe all I needed was you.

Today I hate
realizing the one that I hate is myself.

You sure know how to make a girl cry.

You've mastered it, along with wrapping her around your finger until you are ready to let go.

I do not know what is sicker,
the way you play me,
or the way I let you.

I guess I have mastered my own way
of making a girl cry.

At least I have the decency of only harming myself.

Let Me Fucking Cry

Our love was a chronic consumption.

Eating one another's hearts, hoping it would make our own beat a little more.

Under
my
skin
lie
stories of you
that have yet to be unsurfaced.

-trauma brain

Let Me Fucking Cry

This city used to excite me with the thought of starting this new journey with you. Like we got to hit a reset button. We got older, and I had hoped we would become a bit wiser, even though I could see your feet a decade in the past. But I thought if I reached out my hand long enough, eventually you would find your way back to me. But, I guess you were never really mine to begin with.

-loving a lie for four years

Rhiannon Janae

I was never yours while your pants dropped for others.
As your body fell into others.

I was never yours
because you were everyone else's.

- body counts

Let Me Fucking Cry

Lately, I have been filling my days in the
sunshine.
Headphones in my ears,
thinking about all the ways I love you,
and all the ways I hate you.

Lately, I have been filling my days in the rain.
Headphones in my ears,
thinking about all the ways I hate to love you,
and all the ways I love to hate you.

-oxymoron

A poet gets their best work from their pain.

And that my dear, is why I call you, my muse.

Let Me Fucking Cry

Were their moans just loud enough like mine?
Did they finger your hair as you entered them?
Did their taste leave you gasping for more, as I did?

-monogamy wasn't in his vocabulary

Twin flames do not sit well with me.
Maybe because it is toxic
to be meant for someone else.

And isn't that what we were?
T o x i c,
yet meant for each other?

We loved and hated each other just the same.

Our passion gnawing at my heart like a
hammer to the head.

r e p e a t r e p e a t r e p e a t

I never knew you could miss someone so much,
all while not missing them at all.

Let Me Fucking Cry

Did all your fucks notice my name tattooed on your wrist as you set my calls to silent?

Rhiannon Janae

Kiss me with your silk lips
and forbidden truth inside of them.

Touch me with your bruised fingertips
that brush against charred metal
in the mornings.

You are the kind of guy who smells of cheap
cigarettes and years of heartbreak.

You are the kind of guy
I will live the rest of my life regretting
giving myself to.

-bad boys in black jeans

Let Me Fucking Cry

I want your mistakes to no longer have a home
inside of me.

-eviction notice

I do not understand this path or why I must walk it. I see others smile, and it makes me angry at the realization that the world keeps on turning, yet here I am, still barely moving. Isn't it such a cruel thing, how the world can change in a split second yet, we cannot even pause for a moment?

Let Me Fucking Cry

What makes me hate you the most is the fact
that you would not give us a chance to put our
pieces back together before you broke more off.

-the pieces were me

Rhiannon Janae

Motels and cigarette smoke.

Your kiss sweeping across my lips,
knowing these lips have tasted another woman's
before we checked into this filth.

I swear I lie to myself about how much you love me.
But every time I get myself in your arms, all the bad
runs away.

Because for some reason, the weight of your embrace
shields away the darkness.

But maybe they just capsize me into it.

I am addicted to loving you.

When I am without you, I feel sick.
Yet, when I am with you, I feel even sicker
from the fact that I have let this be the only thing I
want.

-emotional suicide

Let Me Fucking Cry

Forever feels like the biggest lie that has ever left your mouth.

Rhiannon Janae

His arms were around the waist of some girl who didn't even know his favorite color, or how much he loved his back gently scratched as he fell asleep. It was me who always told him how much he was worth and kissed the tears off his cheeks, yet my calls were rushed to silence. I was no longer enough. The silence spoke volumes of how I am no longer wanted or needed. I have become a dead flower, being replaced by fresh-cut daisies. Something you give away, in hopes that one day, someone comes along and sees your worth.

**I scream at his voicemail,
knowing that his mouth is too busy to talk,
and his hands are too full to answer.**

-fool me three times and I am the fool

Let Me Fucking Cry

I can feel a burning inside my chest.
As if someone has hollowed me out
and replaced my insides with an ongoing
flame.

Not the kind of fire
that entices you.

The kind of fire that entraps you in a corner
as you wait for it to capsize you.

I can feel it trickle through my fingertips,
so that all I touch turns to ash.

So I keep my hands in my pockets,
and swear to never love again.

-jaded and faded

Let Me Fucking Cry

I thought
it was you
it was me
it was us
it was all worth fighting for
it was all going to get better
it was all going to be okay.

I thought
we were right
we were real
we were whole
we were the kind of love we've always wanted
we were going to forgive each other
we were going to forgive ourselves.

I thought we were in this together.

-us lives in l-us-t

Let Me Fucking Cry

The game of love you called it,

me being your pawn.

Rhiannon Janae

I never understood how you would tell
everyone how much you loved me behind my
back but kept breaking my heart right in front
of my face.

-the greatest showman

Let Me Fucking Cry

I gave you all my love and you never held it. You never let it fill you up with warmth and comfort. My passion was made to feel welcomed, but your door was always closed. My love was meant for acknowledgment, but you kept your head down and eyes on the ground. My passion was meant for endless years and growing old, but you disappeared into the universe and left dust in your tracks. My love was made to be returned, but you took it and crushed it in your palms to blow to the birds.

-birdfeed

Rhiannon Janae

Everyone used to say how beautiful we looked
together.

Your green eyes,
my blues.

Your brown hair,
my red.

If only they knew how ugly our love was.

-ugly love looks so good on us

Let Me Fucking Cry

My body is my home, and after I saw how you treated your home, I should have known how you would treat my body.

-my body is not your playground

Rhiannon Janae

This anger has caused me blurred visons.

I want to scream so loudly,
but there is no one here to hear me.

I want to cry softly,
but there's no one here to see me.

I want to rip my heart outside of my chest
because all it does is hurt me these days.

I have found ways to hate everything around
me,
because nothing is you.
The funny thing is,
I hate everything besides you,
when you are the one thing I should hate.

Let Me Fucking Cry

I know our love was crazy,
but I like to think it was because
we loved too hard.

We fell apart in each other's hands instead
of mending our own to hold ourselves up.

They say, "Young love makes you stupid."
But many years have passed,
and though I have grown older,
how much wiser have I become?

We were both raised by mothers
who only knew how to put themselves first.

Mothers who only cared about the outside
and not about all the pain they were causing us on
the inside.

-mommy issues

Let Me Fucking Cry

I have become such a shell of a person.
Do I blame me?
Do I blame you?
Or was it both of us?
Throwing around something so rare,
like we knew what the hell we were doing.
Setting fires that we couldn't put out.
Building walls that we couldn't take down.

Taking for granted the one thing we've always
wanted.

Love.

Rhiannon Janae

Our love burned down.
You became ashes,
and I became the flame
that couldn't keep from burning everything
that came along its way.

-rage and regret

Let Me Fucking Cry

Our love has created such a monster inside of me, that sometimes when I least expect it, that monster creeps out from under my chest, and causes serious wounds to those who never cut it.

-anger

Getting lost in the tragedy, instead of
embracing the transition.

Let Me Fucking Cry

You should have loved me the way you would brag to others about how much I loved you. How you wrote me in your life as the hero who kept you alive, all while becoming the villain who recklessly broke my heart into millions of pieces. Cracking more and more at every broken promise or endless self-destruction. You should have loved me the way you painted me as the woman of your dreams, as you became the nightmare of mine. You should have loved me as much I loved you, because that my dear, was

selfless, effortless, wholehearted love

all while you gave me

selfish, reckless, heartless love.

What is causing your anger?

_____

_____

_____

_____

_____

_____

_____

_____

_____

_____

_____

_____

_____

_____

_____

_____

_____

_____

_____

_____

_____

_____

The Bargaining

Let Me Fucking Cry

What would have happened if we had found ourselves before we lost each other?

Where did it all go wrong?

Maybe we loved too hard, too fast.

Maybe we looked inside one another for all the things we never got as children.

Maybe we gave each other the wrong tools to fix ourselves.

Maybe it was the wrong place or the wrong time.

Maybe, we gave each other the only love we knew how to give because it was all we were ever taught.

-*childhood trauma*

Let Me Fucking Cry

Can I beg you for just a sign that your arms are still gently wrapping themselves around my waist? That your wants are still having me there the moment your eyes open in the morning? Can you just play a song that will sing a memory to my ears of one of our favorite times? Can you make these walls talk in the same melody as your voice? Can you send me a message that assures me from wherever you are, that I am still your favorite girl?

-damsel in desperation

Rhiannon Janae

My anger has subsided this week and has yet again been replaced with a longing for you. The cycle of hate and love I have towards you drives me mad. I have thought of locking myself up, but I know you will find a way under the cracks. Why can't I decide how to emotionally digest you? When I hate you, I think how could I have ever loved you? On the days I love you, I think, how can I have so much hate for a ghost?

-talking with a ghost

Let Me Fucking Cry

*Setting fires inside one another in hopes they will
not burn us alive.*

-toxic fumes

It's like I am the air
and you are the fire,
polluting one another
while creating such a glow.

It's like I am the water
and you are the waves,
pulling me under
but holding on
for one last breath.

It's like I am the thunder
and you are the lightning,
following one after the other.

It's like you are the love
and I am the hate.
You cannot feel one
without the other.

Let Me Fucking Cry

I will never understand how some people can
make us feel everything all at once, while
others can make us feel nothing at all.

Rhiannon Janae

I can still smell the scent of lavender
heating up our bedroom.
How the wick lit up your eyes
that had been lost from the light for so long.
I can still feel the calmness floating in the air
and pressing down on my shoulders,
as the weight of morning light
made you sick.
Because once that light shone through our
cracked window,
the light in your eyes would be blown out.

-*morning sickness*

Let Me Fucking Cry

Every birthday you would ask me what I wished for after I blew out the candles. I never told you because I thought it was silly. I did not tell you, because I wanted it to come true. You and I growing old and becoming the kind of love we always said we could be. I wished for you to get better, and for me not to keep getting worse. That was my wish every year for four years. I used to think it never came true, but now I think it may have. Maybe wherever you are, you are becoming the love you always knew you could become. And maybe slowly, I am becoming the love I always knew I could be. And somehow, we are both receiving it from each other without even knowing.

-it's in the air

Rhiannon Janae

At night I shut off all the lights and wait for you
to whisper goodnight.

That is why I have been having a lot of
sleepless nights.

-only silence fills these walls

I want to shove the world into a dark corner and tell it to go **fuck off.** I want to scream out all the ways it has let me down in hopes that somebody hears me and tells me it's all going to be okay. I want to crumble all the mistakes I have made into my palms and watch as they fall through my fingertips as nothing but dirt. I want to ask why I have such a burden to bear when all I asked for was love. I want to understand others' heartbreak without becoming angry with how it doesn't compare to mine. I want to wake up as a version of myself who does not live with this loss etching itself deep inside my heart. I want to see the world for what it can be, and not for all that it has not been.

-let me fucking cry

A haunting;

When someone is no longer here, but you see them in everything.

Let Me Fucking Cry

If I cover my ears with my hands
and bring my knees to my chest
with my eyes closed,
it almost feels like you are here with me.

If I just keep pretending like this,
rocking back and forth,
then maybe I can stay in this trance.

Because I don't care who sees me like this
if it means I'll be able to see you.

My muse,
lace your fingertips through my hair
and tell me I am pretty.

Tie my lips around your waist,
and tell me I am good.

Open my legs
and embrace me
in your danger
by telling me
I am yours.

A man has claimed me
who does not even know himself.

So that when he leaves, (and he will),
no one will know who to look for.

-John Doe

Let Me Fucking Cry

*He's a lover that barely keeps you holding on, but
has you way too scared of letting go.*

Rhiannon Janae

This city once bribed me with hopes, dreams,
and endless opportunities that could open
inside of me.

It promised a home for our love that could be
safe, and maybe a place where you would
finally stay.

But it deceived us,
and its lack of happiness became inevitable.
All that came was pain and barren love.

You did not stay.
In fact, you disappeared forever
in a city I grew to hate.

Now, I ride the train out to the suburbs
where I pretend you are waiting for me
at our old stop,
holding flowers and wearing an apology on
your lips.
Telling me you are sorry for leaving,
or for leading me here at all.

-suburban sorrow

Let Me Fucking Cry

If I could describe our love in one word,
I would use the word wreckage;

a form of disaster,
but a thing one cannot look away from.

Maybe if life could give us
another chance,
another minute,
another second.

Maybe this time we could
do it all right
and take small steps.

Maybe you could keep my hand in yours,
so that if life takes you away,
we could at least say goodbye.

-bargaining

It is a silence you cannot bear ringing in your ears, as the one thing you prayed to never happen, happens. A thing you only see in someone else's tears. But that is the thing about life, it ends. When life takes someone from you, you cannot prepare for the gut punch it breeds inside your stomach. There is no prepping for the scar that it leaves on your heart or the emptiness that it burrows inside your bones. It is that silence ringing in your ears that reminds you of the loss that lies here. We prepare as much as we can, but when death shows up, we lose all the tools we've borrowed. The only thing I could prepare for when I lost you was hangovers.

-disassociating myself for the lack of my sanity

If I could just see your green eyes in the stars in the night sky outside my window, then maybe I could sleep a little bit better.

-insomnia

Let Me Fucking Cry

I am sitting outside your old house again tonight. If I squint my eyes just the right way, I can see you sitting on the porch, cigarette hanging from your fingertips, as your green eyes shine over towards me through the sunset. But it is dark outside now, and I figure my vision is just wine-infused grief.

-drunk talking

Rhiannon Janae

It isn't all the fighting,
or all the steps I took
to walk away
that kill me.

It is the fact that
I no longer
hear your footsteps
following behind me.

-shadow-less

Let Me Fucking Cry

If I could go back,
would I ignore your first phone call?

Or would I stay on the line longer,
making sure I memorized the tone of your
voice?

If I could go back,
would I turn my face away from yours as you
first leaned in to kiss me?

Or would I have found a way to store it away in
a jar for days like this

when I long for your taste.

-kisses in jars

I decided to disappear while at your funeral. I rest my head on the old wooden bench where others have sat vertically, while I lay horizontally. I wonder how many others have cried in this same pew. I wonder how many hearts have been broken in this cheap, scam of a building. I knew you would not want a funeral like this, but it was not in my hands. Nothing was in my hands any longer. I have lost everything I once held onto, including myself. I pray that maybe if I keep crying this hard, my tears will drown me, and I will fall deep under the rockiness of my own waves. Or maybe somehow my tears will sweep me through the stained glass and brush me against your shore. Then, we can walk to the beach that I have not revisited since you have been gone. Maybe if I keep crying, you will feel bad enough to come back for me.

-tear tides

Let Me Fucking Cry

My arms clasped to the back of your ribs,
molding my hands to birth a moonflower
on your back.
Erasing all the heartache that would pave our future
steps.
So that when you left,
all I would see is a moonflower in your dust.

-seeing the beauty in all the pain

Loving you in all the right ways, in all the wrong places.

Darling, where did it all go wrong? What hour, or what day did our thread start to unravel? My lips never left your mouth, but my heart started to dangle through your hands, like some sort of yo-yo. You kept letting me go, knowing I would always come back a little more broken than before.

-pieces of me in your pocket

Rhiannon Janae

I have crawled into a dream
that paints a firefly
on my bedroom wall.

So the dark always sheds light
and the light never dims.

Maybe the way your skin felt like velvet on my
arms was where comfort started to root.

Or maybe it was finally being held by arms that
were truly meant for me.

*Why is it that we feel safest in the arms of the most
dangerous?*

-Stockholm syndrome

Let Me Fucking Cry

Blue daisies fill my palms,
as petals got pulled for the sake of our love.
It always lands on "no".
But I make sure to squeeze the last petal
tightly in my fist,
to threaten it to make my wish come true.
The wish of you holding me in your arms
that no longer hurt me.
The hope of you changing those eyes that look at me
with so much resentment.
I am begging that the next bouquet of blue daisies
that you place in my arms is your final way of
saying,
"I'm sorry, it'll never happen again."

-he loves me, he loves me not

Rhiannon Janae

I hate the beach because it reminds me of you. Everything already reminds me of you, so I must try to avoid some things for the sake of my own sanity. My eyes open in the mornings, and the first thing I see is the emptiness of your side of the bed where you used to leave me. The emptiness of how mornings did not mean the same to you as they did to me, because you were always chasing something that did not love you. Something that in the end, would kill you. If only you had just stayed in bed so that I could have loved you. Then maybe, I could appreciate the ocean and its waves.

-all that I crave is your waves

I felt the ocean last night as I was drowning in your love. I always knew how to swim, but your waves are something vital. They pull me under without taking my last breath away. They pull me to the surface without finding asylum on the shore. I cannot tread in your waters for much longer, because my legs are becoming weak with you in between them. I think if you leave me like this for too long, I will become another abandoned thing that has been lost at sea.

Rhiannon Janae

I once told another man after a couple of
months that I loved him.

I carelessly held his heart and lied to his eyes.

Throwing around those three big words that
still belonged to you.

-lies on my tongue

Let Me Fucking Cry

Since you have left, I have found peace in allowing myself to become a version of myself that I don't like. I have been drowning myself with cheap wine in dive bars, pretending that some boy has my eye. If I keep pretending like this, then maybe I will become this person permanently. So that the old me can die and we can find each other again.

-delusions in dive bars

Please remind me that you are here through the emptiness of my walls. Please touch me with the feeling that somewhere, somehow, we will once again laugh at the way I can't tell jokes. Please assure me through the way the wind blows that you are off somewhere, trying to write a letter that only *I* will find in the falling of the leaves. Please, even if it's only in my dreams, tell me that you still love me.

I started playing music again because I feel that through these lyrics, I can reach you between our different parallels.

Through these chords, I can vibrate through different dimensions.

Through these pages, I feel I can write you back to me.

-magic marker

Rhiannon Janae

I cannot sleep tonight because I can still feel your body heat next to mine. But when I open my eyes to look for you, all I see is the green hoodie you have left me with. It still smells like your cologne and that is why I keep it lying on your pillow where your head used to rest. It comforts me to smell you throughout the night, but then the reality of opening my eyes crushes me. I refuse to wash it since you have left. It is the last smell of you I will ever have. I know the day will come when this green hoodie will no longer carry on the scent of you, and I don't know how I will be able to digest that.

Let Me Fucking Cry

The thing with love is,
we feel it coming,
we feel it leaving,
but forget about it when it is there.

Rhiannon Janae

The ghost in my head has come back,
and I thought the last visit was the end.

This time it's sadness he haunts me with.

How I wish we could have one more laugh
or one more kiss.

Or maybe your fingertips
can trace around my chest
and beg for my heart back.

Even though I believe you still have it,
or at least my old one.
I grew a new one,
but it doesn't beat the same.

It beats fast and causes me to feel out of body.

If only this ghost could leave me be,
maybe then my heart could remain calm.

But the ghost loves me,
and I am a sucker for a haunting.

Let Me Fucking Cry

I was drowning,
my head under water,
but I thought,
if I put all my strength
into saving you,
it would bring my own head
to the surface.

-all I became was an anchor

They say you never forget your first love, but nothing about what happens when they are taken from you as you are still loving them. Maybe the ending wouldn't have led us to the white picket fence, but anything would have been better than this room. This room of stale wooden benches aligning the inside of these religious walls where pictures of you flood the front altars, as the only evidence of your existence. No, see, maybe the ending wouldn't have led us to coffee mornings and goodbye kisses, but I will never forget my first love. Especially when I never got to say goodbye.

-there is no fun in funeral

What is causing you to bargain?

_____

_____

_____

_____

_____

_____

_____

_____

_____

_____

_____

_____

_____

_____

_____

_____

_____

_____

_____

_____

_____

The Depression

Let Me Fucking Cry

Nothing is more innocent than falling in love with someone who has not yet hurt you.

-sinless lovers

Rhiannon Janae

Maybe in a way,
we both used one another, hoping that if we
could dive deep enough inside each other,
we could numb out all that has hurt us.

But as we dove,
we ignored the fact
that the deeper we got,
the more hurt we caused.

-depth to the dagger

Let Me Fucking Cry

You left specks of yourself in my veins.
You always said that was the fastest way to
your heart.

-straight to the heart

Rhiannon Janae

Grief wraps itself around me like a wool blanket in the dead of winter. Warming all over the brokenness that burrows inside this skin of mine. How funny it is to think that the one thing that is always here with us can be the very thing that takes it all away.

-a lack there of

Let Me Fucking Cry

You asked me to save you,
but you were the person who was pulling you under.

It was always two against one.

-against all odds

Rhiannon Janae

I still remember our first kiss.
How my body unfroze for the first time since I
had been alive by just the touch of your lips.

I still remember the night we fell in love.
It was outside of that one shitty bar, and you
said you weren't looking for anything serious.
But you left me in your bed the next morning as
you went to work.

I still remember only seeing you in my future
and how all the pain of losing my mother
disappeared the moment you walked into the
room.

I still remember how we talked for hours,
saying nothing and everything all at the same
time.

I still remember how we found so much
comfort in one another's grief.
And now that you are gone, that grief only sits
inside of me.

-the grief inside of me

Let Me Fucking Cry

Fighting someone else's battle
will only make your own twice as heavy.

Rhiannon Janae

Grief moves inside us so fast,
but stays like a
h a u n t i n g
in an old house.

I walked the city today. The air felt like knives slicing down my spine. The summer hits me like winter's coldest air traveling through my lungs, making breathing become more difficult. I keep looking towards the sun hoping humidity will evaporate me to wherever you are. I don't listen to upbeat music or cruise down the shoreline. I like to think of moments like that with you in them. So, I decided to just walk the city all summer long, becoming everything invisible.

Rhiannon Janae

Fourth of July.
I lied on your chest
as the sky lit up.

I don't remember
which was louder,
the fireworks,
or my heart beating for you.

I always fell apart in your arms,
because your touch never lasted long enough.

And it took just as long
to put myself back together
as it did to fall apart in your arms
all over again.

Let Me Fucking Cry

He could have broken me in half,
but he chose to break me into pieces.

-there's enough of me to go around

Rhiannon Janae

I feel like a walking zombie in this city.

I hide behind make-up that covers these heavy
and sleepless nights
hanging under my eyes.

The nightmare of waking in this heartbreak
reality day after day.

The lack of closure that haunts me in my
waking hours.

The feeling of abandonment that wraps me up
in its arms.

I am surrounded by thousands of people, yet
not one of them can feel my pain, or even know
that I feel it at all.

-*strangers*

Why do we put our hands in fire and wonder why we get burned?

Why do we let our hearts fall for those who do not appreciate our love because they cannot give it to themselves, let alone us?

Why do we listen to the what-ifs and not what has been?

Why do we always find hope in all that is hopeless?

Rhiannon Janae

I want to crawl out of my skin and shed this pain that grows inside of me. Will I feel like this forever? Will I always soak in the black cloud pouring down over my head? Will I ever become sunshine with a clear sky? Will I always be misery, no longer with any company?

-cloudy with a chance of brokenness

Let Me Fucking Cry

They say there is no wrong way to grieve.
So, leave me be;
in this dark lit bar,
soaking in cigarette smoke,
drinking to erase all these memories
that haunt me from the moment my eyes open
in the mornings.

Leave me be,
as I let me go.

My love,

"This time will be different." you say as you back
your body away from me.

The drugs won again.
It is September now.
A whole summer without you.

Your homecoming was wrapped in
promises of sobriety in our tiny apartment
I worked my ass off to rent.

I wish I had never lived there.

I rented it in hopes of loving you in a romance that
was so out of touch with reality, I am ashamed I ever
dreamt it at all.

It was broken and built on neglect,
and those walls have seen a side of you that even you
grew to hate.

Christian street changed me.

Let Me Fucking Cry

You disappeared and I fell through the floorboards
for years.
I let myself get lost, so I did not have to feel the ache
of heartbreak you left me with.

I left the city to find myself.

-Christian Street

Rhiannon Janae

'Till death do us part.
But we never got a chance
because death stole you away
before we could ever tie our fingers together.

-newly-ends

Let Me Fucking Cry

Goodbye Goodbye Goodbye Goodbye Goodbye
Goodbye Goodbye Goodbye Goodbye Goodbye
Goodbye Goodbye Goodbye Goodbye Goodbye
Goodbye Goodbye Goodbye Goodbye Goodbye
Goodbye Goodbye Goodbye Goodbye Goodbye
Goodbye Goodbye Goodbye Goodbye Goodbye
Goodbye Goodbye Goodbye Goodbye Goodbye
Goodbye Goodbye Goodbye Goodbye Goodbye
Goodbye Goodbye Goodbye Goodbye Goodbye
Goodbye Goodbye Goodbye Goodbye Goodbye
Goodbye Goodbye Goodbye Goodbye Goodbye
Goodbye Goodbye Goodbye Goodbye Goodbye
Goodbye Goodbye Goodbye Goodbye Goodbye
Goodbye Goodbye Goodbye Goodbye Goodbye
Goodbye Goodbye

-the only closure I'll ever get

I can feel myself slowly falling out of my own grasp.

Let Me Fucking Cry

How can someone feel this much emptiness
from the loss of another human being?

Just knowing your heart no longer beats makes
me want to rip mine out and stomp all over it.

Knowing I will never hear your voice makes me
want to glue my mouth shut and only swear
silence.

*It is the irony of how I am so incredibly lost, while
you have finally become found.*

Rhiannon Janae

When we first fell in love,
we knew we were both battling wars of trauma.

Though I kept my armor on,

your war still became bigger than the both of
us.

-crossfire

Let Me Fucking Cry

Why does it feel like all my organs are jumbled around inside of me? I guess I feel less than human. Something that is only simply existing, and barely living. I want some sort of peace, but do not know where to find it. This grief has taken over me and all anyone can see are these painted on smiles that I wear to work to pay for this apartment that I no longer want. It still smells like you. I don't know if that makes it better or worse.

Depends on the day.

-my sixth scents

Today marks three years since you have been gone. It feels like just yesterday we watched that one movie over and over because we had no cable. I could never watch the same movie over and over now. I guess it wasn't the movie I was soaking up in those hours. It must have been the silence we were laying in. How just each other's company was enough that day.

Let Me Fucking Cry

I stopped playing music because it reminds me
of the girl I was when you were here, and I am
too scared to feel her.

Rhiannon Janae

Mornings feel like a death sentence for me. Knowing I must get through another day without you here. How I must hold back the pain that builds up behind my eyes. Why do I have to pretend like I am okay when all of me is in pieces held together by tough skin?

-*warrior woman*

Let Me Fucking Cry

Your touch started becoming foreign.
Dissociating myself from your hands.
The ones my neck wore
on that Tuesday night.
Lips swollen,
hovering over an empty bottle of rum.

They say love hurts.

Yes, now I can understand.

-the wall wears my silhouette

Rhiannon Janae

Who can I blame?

The truth is,
I keep breaking my heart
just as badly as you have.

Let Me Fucking Cry

You, five words falling out of your mouth,

"I know how you feel."

Me, five words hanging off my tongue,

"You're someone I could love."

Us, not expecting only one word would be left unsaid,

"Goodbye."

When we ignore our own neglect for so long, we become comfortable in the pain we have created.

Let Me Fucking Cry

Green reminds me of you.
Green eyes, green hoodie, green t-shirt
like the one you wore on your last birthday.

You fell through my fingertips that night
as I held your face against mine.

I should have held on tighter.
If only I knew those were the last candles you
would ever blow out.

-26

Rhiannon Janae

The crack of the door shone a darkness.
One that I knew was there but was always too
scared to face.
When I allowed it in,
all of my nightmares consumed me.
I knew at that moment I had gained
a lot more than I had lost.

-*you have PTSD*

Let Me Fucking Cry

I have changed my hair so many times since you have been gone in hopes that one of these colors will transform me into somebody else. Somebody who does not carry the weight of the failure I have clinging to my back. Because whether my eyes are opened or closed, all that races through my mind is the guilt of not being able to save you; and that is what is eating me alive.

-they call me the caretaker

We become toxic to others when we neglect to give ourselves the love we need.

Let Me Fucking Cry

The difference between love and drugs is:

The drugs did everything to kill you,
but I did everything to keep you alive.

Rhiannon Janae

City blues, wine lips.

I crash into myself every late night.

I don't think this life is made for me.
Or maybe it is the autumn in the air
that reminds me of how we used to celebrate
another year of your birth.

Fall was my favorite,
but now I just crumble into my own hands as
my heart burns at the thought of my own
loneliness.

I cannot drink this hot tea without
remembering who used to boil my water and
stir in the honey.

I have become nothing more than empty
memories that are melting away inside my
head.
I am so scared of the day when I forget the
sound of your voice or how you would hold
my hand in yours.

Let Me Fucking Cry

They say time heals all wounds, but I think
time has caused my wounds to reopen.
You see, everything was not okay with you, but
now it feels even worse without you.
I can only pretend to like these faces that stand
in front of me for so much longer.

I cannot keep drinking these bottles because I
never do find you at the bottom of them.

-I used to be a morning girl

I shouldn't even say that I wish I was someone else, because I don't even know who I am to begin with.

Let Me Fucking Cry

I am not a widow because I never took your
name.

Maybe I am the kind of widow with eight legs
and a deadly bite.

Maybe I am the kind of girl that will make you
fall in love with her and leave you empty-
hearted.

Maybe I am the villain to take the place in this
story now.

Maybe I am the drug you cannot get enough of,
but you know is only killing you from the
inside out.

Or,
perhaps I am just a widow without a name.

I sit here,
in my room,
days on end,
letting my mind
cruelly blame me
for not being able to keep you here.
In this home,
in this room,
in this life.

I think maybe if I hadn't *said that* or didn't *do
this*,
that you would still be standing in the
doorway, hanging your arm above your head
on the doorframe as you laughed at me for how
many outfits I have changed into, only to go
grocery shopping.

I think maybe if I had just kissed your lips a tad
bit longer, then your heart would be too full to
digest yourself with things that only want to
harm you.

But I am here,
alone,

Let Me Fucking Cry

in my room for
days on end,
thinking of all that I didn't do,
and not acknowledging all that I did do.

He was the first one I let inside my bones. He swore I was made for him, like a sweetness he needed to taste on his lips every morning. But his tongue was bitter, so I accustomed my taste to swallow his words. Days became years and I became versions of myself that I no longer enjoyed because I was "made for him". My reflection had gotten lost behind his shadow; and what scared me the most was that I had stopped looking for it.

Let Me Fucking Cry

I was a seed
kept in your palm
starved of water
so I wouldn't outgrow you.

Rhiannon Janae

I remember that day in the park,
in the city that would
soon become our demise.

I laid on your chest under the sunshine,
feeling every beat your heart let out.

The sun was in my eyes,
but you shaded me from it with your hands.

I preferred your chest
as my pillow, always.

But now, all that lies under my head
is a pillow that once laid under yours.

And on sunny days, the sun shines in my eyes.

-depression

Let Me Fucking Cry

The problem with moving on is
wherever you move
it follows.

I watched you change.
Your smile slowly melted off.
Our eyes met a gaze,
but only emptiness hid behind those green eyes of
yours.
That shimmer of hope you held for so long was gone.
I always feared this.
When you would go too far
that you would not be able to get yourself back.
I knew when you looked at me
that Tuesday night at the coffee shop on the corner,
that the person I had loved for so long
was no longer the person that sat in front of me
against the glass window.
Eye to eye.
Blink to stare.

I left my heart on that table that night.

Let Me Fucking Cry

They say,

"Think about all the good times. Let it take away the hurt."

but my eyes have started uncovering themselves.

And now all I'm starting to see is that remembering the **good times** was my way of denying that the bad times were much bigger, and all I end up feeling is sick.

You cannot love the hurt out of someone.
They must love themselves enough in order to
heal.

I do not have skeletons in my closet,
only graves.

You left me with a hole inside of my chest. A huge emptiness that I have been carrying around with me for years. It is a blank sheet of paper that hollows itself around my heart. The lack of closure that I have walked many miles with and screamed plenty of profanities at. It's as if you have given me a book with no words written inside, a movie with no film playing, or music without any sound. I am constantly trying to write you out of me, but there is no pen. My hands do not work, and all I am left with at the end is that blank sheet of paper with only your last words written on it:

"I love you."

What is causing your depression?

_____

_____

_____

_____

_____

_____

_____

_____

_____

_____

_____

_____

_____

_____

_____

_____

_____

_____

_____

_____

_____

_____

_____

The Acceptance

Let Me Fucking Cry

Acceptance is a sign that we are ready to let go of all the things we cannot control, and grab hold of the things that we can.

Rhiannon Janae

The thing with grief is,
it does not go away,
we become adjusted
to living with it.

But sometimes when it's quiet,
I open the part of me
where the grief lies,

and tell it to go **fuck off.**

Let Me Fucking Cry

When I met him,
I let him consume me.
I wanted all of him
filling me up inside.
I wanted only his love
in my skin,
in my bones
and in my blood.
I let him fill me up so high
that I had no room left inside
for myself.

-my self-less-love

I saw my mother
in his eyes.

The same sadness
and silence
trapped their voices.

I thought maybe this time
if I loved him enough,

I could save them both.

But my mother had been gone
and the problem was not the lack of my love
that took them both.
It was the lack of love they had for themselves.

That was the silent killer.

We became lost in love because we believed that we could not live without one another. Not understanding that both of us had been lost the whole time, and our love kept us even farther apart from ourselves than before our lips had ever touched.

-recklessly in love

Rhiannon Janae

Be careful of lovers full of self-destruction,
because their self-harm will one day become your
burden.

Let Me Fucking Cry

Broken doesn't always look like a bunch of
shattered pieces flooding the floor.

Broken looks like sleepless nights or sleeping
all day.

Broken looks like downing cheap bottles of
wine and stumbling home at 1 a.m.

Broken looks like sinking into the bathtub, as
the water devours your head in hopes of
shutting your mind off.

Broken looks like painted-on smiles as your
insides wilt.

Broken can often look a lot like beauty.

Rhiannon Janae

That phone call nearly killed me.
My spirit exited itself,
but kept my body in sight.
My heart fell out
and I left it there,
hoping it would hurt less,
but it hurt all the same
for years.
Maybe even still,
I can't tell somedays.
I'm in love again,
but it is different
because this love is good for me.
Not like your love
that left me crippled, hovering over myself,
heartless.

I cannot blame him for loving me so recklessly. I can only blame myself for continuing to let these bruises appear on my heart, which was only trying to heal.

Rhiannon Janae

I can still feel you there,
inside my heart.
But I've moved you to a place
somewhere in the back.
So, when I need you,
I can find you there.
But I have now learned,
whoever wants to get inside my heart
must go through all the love I have for myself
to make it in.

Let Me Fucking Cry

Just fucking cry and
let
out
the
hurt.

It makes you
stronger
when
you
take
control
of
your
emotions
and
not
let
them
control
you.

Rhiannon Janae

We fall in love with the version of ourselves
that we see in other people that need the most
healing.

Let Me Fucking Cry

I read our old emails last night and it made me feel so many different emotions simultaneously. Sad, sick, happy and disappointed, all in a matter of seconds. I hated you in some ways and loved you in others. It made me remember who you were and who you were not. It made me remember who I was and who I am not. Some of the words you said to me made me so angry at myself, because now if I saw those words written to me, I would just hit delete. I would make sure you knew who you were talking to and who you were losing. But isn't that the funny thing, that I am starting to find myself after losing you?

Some lovers are temporary but will forever be
a lesson learned.

Let Me Fucking Cry

Queens don't wear crowns.
They wear grief inside their bones and scars on their
hearts.

I had held him in my hands for years after his father's death. Carrying his pain on my back, brushing his ears with hope. But his grief was too heavy. In the end, the burden was too much to bear, and his father's arms were the ones he needed to fall into the most.

Let Me Fucking Cry

I can now see that you loved me the only way
you knew how to while trying to fight battles
inside yourself.

So, I decided to start loving myself in all the
ways you couldn't.

-finding forgiveness

I want to learn how to embrace this grief but not let it cripple me. I hope this grief will throw some pity on me and release me from its grasp. I have held this grief for years now, but I am ready to look it in the eye and not feel my bones shake or my heart burn. I will find peace in loss and peace in grief. It will now strengthen these bones and fill my heart with acceptance. Death will no longer paralyze me because death is inevitable. I can no longer live my life fearing the inevitable, because then I miss opportunities. I must keep growing and not fear. I must not feel dead while living. I must start to live and accept fate for what it is.

-something to help the pain

Let Me Fucking Cry

When I lost my mother
it stung,
but you patched me up
like a band aid.

When I lost you,
it ripped off.

I let it bleed for years.

-open wound

Photographs of you once made me feel comfortable, but comfort is not always what is best for us. It is a safe zone that kept me in the un-comfort of knowing you. I was too scared to let go because I was too frightened of who I would uncover, and all the hate *she* had for me.

-evidence

If you are recovering from someone who has caused the kind of pain that makes it hard to move your body, but even harder to sit still, just know that those who find hope in hopelessness become the version of strength that others will only envy.

Here is a reminder to embrace all the parts of you that others hurt. Because if we let ourselves neglect the aspects of us that need the most healing, we continue letting others hurt us, which makes us just as guilty.

My mother taught me to love with all of me, but I no longer want to love like that. I want to love the same amount as the other. I want to meet someone halfway and encourage each other to not let go of ourselves. And maybe that is where it all went wrong. Loving someone with all of you. Because you see, when that happens, we have nothing left for ourselves.

-no-dependent

Rhiannon Janae

Breaking by the hands of someone else is how
I will never lose my pieces again.

Let Me Fucking Cry

My hands fall to my sides
as my head drops to my chest.
I realized that keeping you stitched together for so
many years has caused my own seams to unthread.

-unraveling

Rhiannon Janae

Maybe next time we meet
we will not dive right into the shallow side,
because that's how things get broken.

Maybe next time, we can gradually
tread in deep waters, slowly making sure
that when we get there,
we can both stand on our own two feet.

-six-feet-under

Let Me Fucking Cry

The disaster started when I realized that I love you more than I love myself.

The disaster ended when you realized you love me more than you love yourself.

Rhiannon Janae

Our arms are only supposed to carry the person they belong to.

Let Me Fucking Cry

Though my mother lost herself too soon,
I like to imagine her on this paper,
writing herself through my fingertips
with this pen.

I like to think I am becoming all that she could
not, saying all that she did not,

being all that she was not.

-mother

Rhiannon Janae

It took me this long to love myself the way I was begging others to. The disappointment and emptiness I had been left with was from my own neglect. Since I have taken the time to get to know myself, I wake up with the warmth of butterflies in my stomach. I now have found a love that genuinely wants the best for me.

Myself.

We are more than what has happened to us.
We just need to live through it in order to figure
that out.

I let myself go for years after I lost you. I became a foreign sight to my own eyes. I hid behind cheap bottles and fake friends. I let my eyes close during blackouts almost every night. I thought if I had lost you, then I must lose myself. I could still hear the pace of your footsteps in the hallway that led to my bedroom. I knew it seemed impossible, but I liked to think it was you watching over me because I was too reckless to watch over myself. I liked to think that maybe seeing me like that showed you how much I missed you. But now when I look back, I realize I was missing myself long before I missed you.

-the ghost inside me

Let Me Fucking Cry

Battles are constant.
We win some.
We lose some.
But we never stop fighting.

Rhiannon Janae

Be kind to your heart. Listen to the way it beats and feel the way it breaks. Give it the rest and patience it needs to mend. The heart holds us together, and we owe it the same love we allow ourselves to give to others. Sometimes our bodies tell us that we need to pay closer attention to the feelings that alarm us. Mending a broken heart is a sign of growth. One moment you feel as if you are never going to be able to make it through, and the next moment you've not only made it, but you shine brighter. Our hearts may break, but they will not be shattered forever.

Let Me Fucking Cry

My twenties were mainly meant for everyone other than myself.

My youth was stolen because I knowingly gave it away on a silver platter for a man to eat.

I guess maybe all my heartache happened so young in hopes that the older I got, the more peace I would receive, or maybe it is just as simple as my own self-sabotage.

Maybe finally, I am learning how to accept love for myself.

Maybe this is what letting go feels like.

Reminder:

Loving someone at their worst should not be at the expense of yourself. There is a difference between accidental behavior and recurring behavior.

What if we were not all the things that happened to us?

What if we were not the abuse or neglect that has scarred us?

What if we were not the bad dreams and the breakdowns?

What if we were the tiny victories and the little smiles?

What if it was not about what the past has done, but about what the future will do?

What if we wrote the story and did not let the story write us?

*One of the most terrifying things I have ever felt in
my life was when I became a stranger to myself.*

Let Me Fucking Cry

Yes, I know our love failed in this lifetime.
But I swear, sometimes when the wind brushes against my cheek, I can feel you kiss me slightly and whisper in my ear that our love has never been stronger.

What I regret the most is longing for the version of myself that I was before him. I lost myself for years looking backwards and ignoring that light up ahead of my blindness. Because in the end, I was too scared of finding the person up ahead because I knew she was a lot stronger than I was at that moment. I knew she would grab me by my arms and shake off all the hurting inside of me and tell me to "get on." I was not scared of the past; I feared the future. The future holds a sign of moving on and that was something my fear could not bear. So, I stayed stagnant for years with my head turned behind me, avoiding the waving arms that were up ahead. Until one day I sat up and said, "Fuck it." and I looked forward and started walking. That was the day I lost and found myself all in the same moment.

-from moth to butterfly

Let Me Fucking Cry

I hope you find beauty in the eyes of the one
who stares back at you in the reflection you
tend to be most afraid of.

Rhiannon Janae

I dreamt of you last night.

You were wrapped in black velvet.

Too soft to touch,
yet too beautiful to resist.

Those sharp green eyes sliced through me
like clean glass
right through my skin.

Your voice was of a lilac cry, echoing through a field
of poppy seeds.

You begged for me to complete you as you dragged
your fingertips up and down my spine.

I felt summoned.

I could not choose you because I can no longer
sacrifice the little girl inside of me who has been
abandoned.

She screams for a home that stays where it is built.

Let Me Fucking Cry

*I could not choose you because your heart is too
flooded to absorb any of my love.
 I could not choose you because of all your empty
promises and lack of appearances.*

*I could not choose you because you wanted to own
me, and I am not one to be tamed.*

I am wild and stubborn.

*I only call to my own wisdom that I have gathered
throughout my years.*

I am raw and righteous.

I am neither here nor there.

I belong to no one.

I belong to the sun.

-sun queen

Rhiannon Janae

I knew I was healing the moment the sun
kissed my face and the wind tangled my hair,
as I thanked myself for choosing to still be here.

I used to think death was something to fear. Until one day, I heard my mother's faint voice in the silence of my walls. I swear I could hear her say,

"It isn't death you are fearing, it is life. You have been asleep in the darkness for too long, but now it is time to return to the light."

It was at that moment I realized that what I had feared the most was the one thing that would make me the happiest: *healing*.

Rhiannon Janae

I find peace in tidal waves, because without them, I would never have learned how to sail.

-swimming through oceans of grief

Let Me Fucking Cry

It was in the moment I found myself halfway under my blanket, raging in excess heartbeats and shallow breaths, that I decided to stop simply existing, and start living.

In the grand scheme of it all, what makes me the sickest is the way I let go of myself repeatedly. It was as if my fingers were made for someone else. It was as if my life was a life I was living for others, trying to control all their pain while increasing my own. I was blind to the fact that what saddened me was the lack of life I had created for myself. The day I lost myself was when I had become broken. The day I lost you was when I stopped blaming you for what I was responsible for this whole time.

Let Me Fucking Cry

I am
in love now,
with the girl who first held me
the night I found out I had lost you.

I like to think
that was your way
of saying goodbye,
while showing me
what I always deserved.

-the calm in the chaos

Rhiannon Janae

Don't push against the current.

Let its waves take you to where you are supposed to be.

Let Me Fucking Cry

I used to bathe in grief. I used to let my self-pity take control of me. I would lash out at the grief with anger and malice. Now I have learned that when grief shows up, to welcome it in, sit with it for a while, then walk it out. Grief can pass through, but it no longer has a home inside of me.

-acceptance

What will help you with acceptance?

_____

_____

_____

_____

_____

_____

_____

_____

_____

_____

_____

_____

_____

_____

_____

_____

_____

_____

_____

_____

Any leftovers?
Leave them here:

_____

_____

_____

_____

_____

_____

_____

_____

_____

_____

_____

_____

_____

_____

_____

_____

_____

_____

_____

_____

Made in the USA
Las Vegas, NV
25 July 2023

75208402R00152